MARRIAGE THAT MATTERS

31 Days That Will Transform Your Relationship

Dr. Emory Berry, Jr.

Sermon To Book
www.sermontobook.com

Marriage That Matters / Emory Berry, Jr.
ISBN-13: 9780692605394
ISBN-10: 0692605398

I would like to thank God for seeing greater in me than I ever could have imagined. In many ways, this book represents the composite of my experiences, education, and exposure in life. Although I am a huge proponent for formal education, I must admit most of the lasting lessons I have learned on this journey were gained outside the classroom. Therefore, I thank my mother, Julie L. Berry, who was my first teacher and my late father, Emory Berry, Sr., who made me feel that I could do anything. So much appreciation is owed to my brothers, Julius and Connally, who have embodied and modeled brotherhood to the highest degree. To my wife, Julie, who is my biggest encourager and helped to refine my rough edges: you are my "diamond and pearl." To my son, Emory III, and daughter, Jaiden: thank you for loving Daddy unconditionally and for sharing me with so many. You all are the motivation for all I do. To my grandparents and ancestors who paved the way for me: thank you! I've tried to build upon your sacrifices and create a legacy for the generations to follow. Thank you to members of Fourth Baptist Church, whom I've had the pleasure of serving, leading, and pastoring. Finally, to every mentor, teacher, counselor, friend, and family member who has encouraged me: THANK YOU!

CONTENTS

Note from the Author

Thank you for purchasing *Marriage That Matters*. This daily devotional is meant to offer couples practical advice, biblical insights, and encouragement to help you experience marriage as God intended.

To assist you in getting the most out of your reading, each chapter includes not only a focus scripture and devotional prayer but reflective questions and a brief action step. I recommend you go through these sections with a pen in order to write your thoughts in the areas provided. In order to maximize your book reading experience, try going through the questions by yourself, with your spouse, or with a study group.

However you choose to approach this book and the accompanying questions, I truly hope you and your spouse will grow in your marital relationship as a result of this reading and in your relationship with Christ.

Your Marriage Won't Be the Same

The ultimate basis of human delight and agony is found in the theatrics that accompanies love and relationships. Marriage has always been the most common context for this drama. Many question the sustainability and rationality of marriage and wonder if it should remain as the core of contemporary societal progression.

If we get rid of the traditional institution of marriage, what will replace it? What more efficient and effective arrangement could we discover to secure the level of assurance, allegiance, sustenance, sense of belonging and affection essential to meeting the basic needs of a human being? How will the needs such as adoration, sense of community, significance, safety, and shared respect be met? Over the past six thousand years, no civilization or culture has fashioned a better notion for systematic social growth than that of the traditional institution of marriage.

We are a pastor and wife and really want this book to help God's people. This book is written with the hope you will find it biblically accurate, emotionally optimistic, practically helpful, and sociologically feasible. Don't read this book being a critic of yourself and your relationship; don't read sections and say to your spouse, "I told you so"; don't say, "I've tried this and it doesn't work." Instead, read this book and take inventory on what is positive in your relationship and how you can move toward a more healthy and meaningful partnership with your spouse.

Marriage that Matters is a resourceful way to check the gauge of your relationship and identify those hidden potholes along the way. Use the next thirty-one days to transform your understanding of marriage.

– Dr. Julie A. Berry

CHAPTER 1

Playing as a Team

One of the beauties of playing sports is that you can play on a team with a group of individuals who have never played together, yet can potentially win the game. One of the primary reasons for this "winning wonder" points to four important facts. First, they understand the importance of following a game plan. Second, they recognize that each individual brings a unique skillset to the team. Third, they realize that it is critical for each individual to play their specific position. And finally, they place great emphasis on playing and competing as a team.

Believe it or not, this "winning formula" can also be applied to Christian marriages. First, couples must remember that the Word of God is God's game plan. Second, couples must determine their individual strengths and weaknesses. Third, couples must agree to carry out specific functions in their marriage. Finally, husbands and wives must commit to playing as a team.

Today, focus on strengthening your marriage by "playing as a team". Remind yourself that you and your spouse are on the same team and what affects "you" affects "them." You will find that by developing this mindset/mentality, you will ultimately become closer to your spouse. Today, *do* something special for your spouse! V*ocalize y*our excitement about being their teammate and the joy you feel from being on the same team as them.

Prayer

Dear God, I would like to thank you for placing my spouse in my life. Thank you for our partnership, uniqueness, and similarities. Help me to be a better team player and help us to fulfill your purpose. Furthermore, allow us to have fun together as our lives bring you glory. In Jesus' name. Amen!

Scripture Focus

*"...and the two will become one flesh. So they are no longer two, but one flesh. — **Mark 10:8 (NIV)***

WORKBOOK

Chapter 1 Questions

Question: Today's reading, made me think about...

_____

_____

_____

_____

_____

_____

_____

_____

_____

_____

_____

Question: My spouse can count on me as a teammate by doing a better job of...

_____

_____

_____

_____

_____

_____

_____

_____

_____

_____

_____

_____

Action: *Vocalize* your excitement about being your spouse's teammate and the joy you feel from being on the same team as them.

Chapter 1 Notes

_____

_____

_____

_____

_____

_____

_____

_____

_____

_____

_____

_____

_____

_____

_____

_____

_____

_____

_____

_____

_____

_____

CHAPTER 2

Win as a Team

There are some who would tell you life pivots around two letters, the letters "W" and "L." For those who are familiar with sports, they would tell you "W" stands for wins and "L" stands for losses. Hence, the goal for many people in life is to have more wins than losses. The reality is, we all will experience losses and we all will experience wins. However, when you play a team sport you quickly recognize you are no longer an individual but part of a team. Inasmuch, you lose as a team and win as a team. In fact, I love to see post-game interviews with athletes who don't take all the credit but thank their team. In the same breath, it is always counterproductive for an individual athlete to place all the blame on their team.

In the same manner, your marriage pivots around your ability to win as a team with your spouse. Not only do you have the capacity to be winners, you were put together by God to be winners. So many marriages dissolve and end in divorce because couples have lost sight of the fact that they are a team. What affects one, affects all. Make a decision today to reverse the trends of failed Christian marriages. Take responsibility for your choices and your relationship. Don't play blame games. Make every effort to win as a couple so future generations will have an example of what a winning marriage looks like.

Prayer

Dear Heavenly Father, thank you for setting my heart on fire today. I truly want to have a winning marriage. Help my spouse and I to be better team players. We look to you for guidance, direction, and patience. Allow our marriage to be an example for future generations. Cancel out every ploy, plan, and plot by the devil to destroy my marriage. Today, I decree and declare victory for my marriage! In Jesus' name. Amen!

Scripture Focus

*The Lord God said, "It is not good for the man to be alone. I will make a helper suitable for him." — **Genesis 2:18 (NIV)***

WORKBOOK

Chapter 2 Questions

Question: Today's reading, made me think about…

_____

_____

_____

_____

_____

_____

_____

_____

_____

_____

_____

Question: One thing I learned today is…

_____

_____

_____

_____

_____

_____

_____

_____

_____

_____

_____

_____

Action: With your spouse, discuss some of the challenges you face and how each of you can best contribute to the team effort in these aspects of life. Be sure to make communication and cooperation part of your plan!

Chapter 2 Notes

_____

_____

_____

_____

_____

_____

_____

_____

_____

_____

_____

_____

_____

_____

_____

_____

_____

_____

_____

_____

_____

_____

CHAPTER 3

Keeping Up with the Joneses

Marriage is a beautiful thing! Three of the benefits of being married is you will experience the blessing of God's first institution, become closer friends with your spouse, and you will enjoy the friendship of other married couples. However, one of the challenges for many marriages is the insatiable temptation to compare your marriage to other marriages. Therefore with this reality in mind, you are charged today to accept the fact that each marriage is unique and distinct. Hence, the uniqueness of your marriage should be valued more, treasured more, and celebrated more.

Who cares if the Joneses (a fictitious last name for people you compare yourself to) get a new car, a new TV, new furniture, or a new home? Do not think other couples represent the perfect couple. Your job is not to compare or compete with the Joneses but to be the best couple you can be, with the Lord's help. However unbeknownst to you and your spouse, you are the

"Joneses'" for some other married couple. You may not be aware of it but some other couple is looking at your marriage. They are observing, watching, and noticing every detail of your marriage. Although it is hard to do at times, see the worth in your own marriage. In every marriage, you will identify areas that are stronger than others and weaker than others. If you and your spouse focus your daily energy on making your strengths stronger and making your weaknesses better, you will not have time to focus on the Joneses.

Today focus on being grateful for "who" the Lord has blessed you with and "what" the Lord has blessed you with. Don't compare yourself to the couple to the left and don't compete with the couple to your right, but keep working on the couple in the mirror. In doing so, expect God to make your marriage more rewarding than it has ever been.

Prayer

Thank you, thank you, thank you God for blessing our marriage the way you see fit. I believe by faith that everything we will ever need, you will provide. In Jesus' name. Amen!

Scripture Focus

...for I have learned, in whatsoever state I am, therewith to be content. — ***Philippians 4:11 (KJV)***

WORKBOOK

Chapter 3 Questions

Question: Today's reading, made me think about...

_____

_____

_____

_____

_____

_____

_____

_____

_____

_____

Question: My spouse can count on me doing a better job to cherish our marriage by...

_____

_____

_____

_____

_____

_____

_____

_____

_____

_____

_____

_____

Action: Celebrate the strengths in your marriage and be intentional to work on the weaknesses in your marriage.

Chapter 3 Notes

_____

_____

_____

_____

_____

_____

_____

_____

_____

_____

_____

_____

_____

_____

_____

_____

_____

_____

_____

_____

_____

_____

CHAPTER 4

Take Out the Garbage

"What's that smell?" Have you ever found yourself asking this question as you entered your kitchen? Don't be ashamed or embarrassed to admit you have asked this question at least once. The reality is our kitchens are not always spaces filled with the scent or aroma of great cooking. However, all of our kitchens are at times spaces which are filled with the odor and stench of garbage that needs to be taken out. With this dichotomy of smells in mind, the household chore of taking out our garbage should remind us there are some things that need to be dismissed, removed, and even thrown away in our marriages.

In every marriage, there will be seasons when the air is not filled with the "aroma of flowers" but filled with the "stench of garbage" that needs to be removed. This stench could be such things as grudges or unforgiveness. Consider these three steps to rid the "stench" of the past in your relationship. First, admit there is a problem/stench. Second, address the problem/stench. Finally, alleviate the problem/stench by moving forward. Sometimes these steps can be accomplished over the course of a single conversation or over the course of several conversations. Do yourself and your spouse a favor by taking out the trash and moving forward. If we are honest, no one likes the smell of old trash because it negatively impacts the most beautiful places and spaces. When the trash in the kitchen is not taken out, its stench eventually permeates the whole house. Don't allow the garbage or stench of past events affect the present or future possibilities of your marriage.

Prayer

Dear God, today I'm praying you will help me let go of grudges and all areas of unforgiveness in my heart. Allow me to free my mind, heart, and soul. I pray to be filled with hope, forgiveness, and love. Please expand my capacity to see beyond yesterday and allow me to dream of an immeasurable future with my spouse. In Jesus' name. Amen!

Scripture Focus

I count not myself to have apprehended: but this one thing I do, forgetting those things which are behind, and reaching forth unto those things which are before, I press toward the mark for the prize of the high calling of God in Christ Jesus. — Philippians 3:13-14 (KJV)

WORKBOOK

Chapter 4 Questions

Question: Today's reading made me think about...

_____

_____

_____

_____

_____

_____

_____

_____

_____

_____

_____

Question: One thing I learned today is...

_____

_____

_____

_____

_____

_____

_____

_____

_____

_____

_____

_____

Action: Share with you spouse one thing from the past you are letting go of and one item from the past you would like them to let go.

Chapter 4 Notes

CHAPTER 5

Walking Side by Side

Shopping malls and shopping plazas can be tons of fun, especially when you have great shopping partners and unrestricted funds to spend. In the same breath, shopping malls and shopping plazas can be great places to indulge in "people watching." "People watching" can be described as the casual act of observing and noticing the behavior of people, namely strangers in a public place. With this definition in mind, have you ever observed or noticed a couple in the mall who did not walk side by side but instead one partner walked in front of the other? Most of us would agree that this behavior might be seen by many as odd, strange, or even peculiar.

I utilize this visual image to metaphorically illustrate the fact that in so many marriages, there are couples who do not walk side-by-side in various parts of their relationship. Unfortunately, too many marriages suffer because couples are not walking side-by-side with their spouse in key areas of their relationship. The dangerous outcome of this disjointed approach to marriage usually results in a lack of regard for the other person's input or influence on various decisions such as finances, parenting, healthcare, careers, etc. Today, I challenge you to ask yourself these questions, "Do I walk side-by-side with my spouse in our marriage? Does my spouse walk behind or ahead of me in key parts of our marriage? Are we willing to respect each other's choices?"

Like the couples you observe when "people watching" at the shopping mall, take a moment to observe your own marriage and identify two areas in your marriage you would like to work on.

Prayer

Dear Gracious God, help me to walk side-by-side with my spouse. Also help my husband/wife to "walk together" and "be agreed" with me for many years to come! In Jesus' name. Amen!

Scripture Focus

Can two walk together, except they be agreed? — *Amos 3:3 (KJV)*

WORKBOOK

Chapter 5 Questions

Question: Today's reading, made me think about...

_____

_____

_____

_____

_____

_____

_____

_____

_____

_____

_____

Question: One thing I learned today is...

_____

_____

_____

_____

_____

_____

_____

_____

_____

_____

_____

_____

Action: See your spouse as your equal! Write down one area in which you have not been walking side by side with them. Make a commitment to do better in this specific area.

_____

_____

_____

_____

Chapter 5 Notes

CHAPTER 6

Add a Little Seasoning

Have you ever made reservations at a nice restaurant in anticipation of a delicious meal? In the same breath, have you ever been disappointed by the bland food of said restaurant? Unfortunately, all of us have experienced meals where the taste of the food was pale in comparison to the air, atmosphere, and ambiance of the restaurant. In these instances, one can't help but wonder "why didn't the owners take the same interest and investment in the food as they did in the facility?" In short, adding a little seasoning to the food could go a long way.

Just as food in many fancy restaurants could use a little seasoning, the same is true for some marriages. So many marriages have become so disappointedly bland that they have forgotten what a seasoned marriage is like. I want to suggest one of the areas that is lacking seasoning in many marriages is the romance department. Unfortunately, the romance department in many marriages go lacking due to the complexities and complications of life.

So the question of the day is "Could your marriage use a little seasoning in the romance department?" Regardless of your response, every marriage could benefit from a little more seasoning in its romance department. Today, begin planning one step you will take to add a little seasoning to the romance department of your relationship. It doesn't have to be long and involved. It could simply be preparing a special meal, sending a random text message saying "I love you", or placing a small piece of chocolate somewhere for them to find later that day. In the end, you will notice an overall improvement in your marriage and your spouse will thank you for it.

Prayer

Lord, today I need your Spirit to help me get out of my comfort zone. I believe you sent my spouse to me and I want to honor that. Please give me a creative idea today that would add seasoning to my marriage. In Jesus' name. Amen!

Scripture Focus

Your love delights me, my treasure, my bride. Your love is better than wine, your perfume more fragrant than spices.
— *Song of Solomon 4:10 (NLT)*

WORKBOOK

Chapter 6 Questions

Question: Today's reading, made me think about...

_____
_____
_____
_____
_____
_____
_____
_____
_____
_____
_____

Question: One thing I learned today is...

_____
_____
_____

_____

_____

_____

_____

_____

_____

_____

_____

_____

Action: Do something spontaneously intimate with your spouse tonight. Pleasantly surprise him or her and enjoy the big smile on their face.

Chapter 6 Notes

_____

_____

_____

_____

_____

_____

_____

_____

_____

_____

_____

_____

_____

_____

_____

_____

_____

_____

_____

_____

_____

_____

_____

_____

_____

CHAPTER 7

Check the Smoke Detector

Fire departments all around the country regularly encourage residents to check the functionality of their home's smoke detectors. Research shows when smoke detectors work properly, they help to save thousands of lives. The purpose of smoke detectors is to alert residents or occupants of the presence of smoke and even fire. If you have ever heard the blaring alarm of a smoke detector, you know it is almost impossible to ignore, disregard, or discount it.

Just as smoke detectors alert us of potential danger in our homes or places of business, it is important to pay attention to the "detectors" that alert us when something is wrong in our marriage. These alerts are communicated to us in so many ways and we must be sensitive to them. What type of alerts is your spouse sending you that you may be missing? What conversation topics does your spouse bring up frequently? Can you name the common complaints or critiques your spouse has about you? As you consider these questions, use them as signals, signs, and warnings that "smoke" or "fire" might be nearby in your marriage. Always remember, the devil loves to take small issues and make them big issues. Hence, don't forget to check your relationship smoke detector.

Prayer

Thank you Creator for creating me to be dynamic. Thank you for giving me the ability to send messages and to receive messages. Today, I ask that you sensitize my spiritual antenna to discern the alerts that my spouse and you are sending me regarding my marriage. Help me to not only detect these alarms but help me take the necessary actions to bring bliss and wholeness to our union. In Jesus' name. Amen!

Scripture Focus

Be of sober spirit, be on the alert. Your adversary, the devil, prowls around like a roaring lion, seeking someone to devour. — 1 Peter 5:8 (NASB)

WORKBOOK

Chapter 7 Questions

Question: Today's reading, made me think about…

_____

_____

_____

_____

_____

_____

_____

_____

_____

_____

_____

_____

Question: One thing I learned today is…

_____

_____

_____

_____

_____

_____

_____

_____

_____

_____

_____

_____

Action: Identify the item or area in your marriage that might be "smoking." This smoke is more than likely a warning that something is about to burn, if not addressed.

Chapter 7 Notes

_____

_____

_____

_____

_____

_____

_____

_____

_____

_____

_____

_____

_____

_____

_____

_____

_____

_____

_____

_____

_____

_____

_____

_____

CHAPTER 8

In-Laws, Out-Laws, or In-Loves

It is true! It has been said "when you marry your spouse, you also marry your spouse's family." Interestingly when you think about this statement, you will find there is some truth to this claim. The truth is, when you married your spouse, you married a lot of the components that makes them who they are. By marrying them, you marry their genetic history, educational history, work history, religious history, psychological history, family history, and the list goes on. For these reasons, it is always important to learn as much as you can about these components of your in-laws history. Understanding these details which are connected to your spouse may help you understand your spouse's actions, attitudes, and perspectives on life.

Specifically, it is important to learn as much as possible about your in-laws. Regardless of your spouse's relationship with them, your in-laws directly and indirectly impact your spouse's life. Unfortunately, there are many instances when marriages struggle because of one's relationships with their in-laws, which some have renamed as "out-laws." In the same breath, it is always healthy for you to support and encourage your spouse to maintain a healthy relationship with their family. There are some instances when it is best for you or your spouse to love your in-laws from afar and then there are instances when in-laws should be loved up close.

Prayer

Dear all-wise God, thank you for the marriage covenant that I share with my husband/wife. Today I pray for my in-laws and ask that you bring harmony where there is division. Help me to see my "in-laws" as "in-loves" and not my "out-laws." Strengthen, fortify, and build us up. In your precious Son's name. Amen!.

Scripture Focus

Therefore shall a man leave his father and his mother, and shall cleave unto his wife: and they shall be one flesh. — **Genesis 2:24 (KJV)**

WORKBOOK

Chapter 8 Questions

Question: Today's reading, made me think about…

_____

_____

_____

_____

_____

_____

_____

_____

_____

_____

_____

_____

Question: One thing I learned today is…

_____

_____

_____

_____

_____

_____

_____

_____

_____

_____

_____

_____

Action: Sit down with your spouse and intentionally decide to do something nice or thoughtful for one of your in-laws.

Chapter 8 Notes

_____

_____

_____

_____

_____

_____

_____

_____

_____

_____

_____

_____

_____

_____

_____

_____

_____

_____

_____

_____

_____

_____

_____

_____

CHAPTER 9

Hot or Cold Coffee

Who would have ever guessed twenty years ago that coffee shops would be as popular as they are today? For that matter, who would ever have guessed coffee shops would be as profitable as they are today? Nonetheless, time has taught us that coffee shops are here to stay and aren't going anywhere. To this point, if you were to visit one of your neighborhood coffee shops, you might be amazed by the expansive and extensive menu which includes hot and cold coffee.

Despite the vast array of options available to customers, most consumers are very predictable and order the same menu item with every visit. Just like many of our predictable visits to the coffee shop, many of us become very predictable in our relationships. Today, I want to challenge you to resist the temptation of being predictable with your spouse. Surprise them, astonish them, and shock them by doing something fun and unanticipated. Hence, by being unpredictable you will add some pizazz to your relationship. You will find that spontaneity will help increase and intensify the fire and passion you and your spouse share. Besides, why stick with only one flavor when you could be strengthening your relationship with spontaneous fun.

Prayer

Dear Sustainer of Life, I am reminded that you are often doing new and exciting things in my life. Today, give me a creative idea that will add some healthy excitement to my marriage. In the Savior's name I pray. Amen!

Scripture Focus

A merry heart doeth good like a medicine: but a broken spirit drieth the bones. — ***Proverbs 17:22 (KJV)***

WORKBOOK

Chapter 9 Questions

Question: Today's reading, made me think about...

_____

_____

_____

_____

_____

_____

_____

_____

_____

_____

_____

Question: One thing I learned today is...

_____

_____

_____

_____

_____

_____

_____

_____

_____

_____

_____

_____

Action: Surprise your spouse and take them to a local coffee shop to simply talk and to have some down time. It may feel weird, but it will be time well spent.

Chapter 9 Notes

_____

_____

_____

_____

_____

_____

_____

_____

_____

_____

_____

_____

_____

_____

_____

_____

_____

_____

_____

_____

_____

_____

_____

_____

CHAPTER 10

Shoes, Sandals, Sneakers, and Slippers

If you have ever experienced a foot massage or pedicure, you quickly learned that stress can be released through your feet. So often we place great attention on our hands and minimal attention on our feet. Podiatrists will tell you your feet absorb your total body weight, help to maintain your balance, and possess some of the smallest blood vessels in the human body. The unfortunate reality is our feet are the furthest extremity from our eyes. However, our feet are often neglected and out of sight. Hence, the old adage of "out of sight, out of mind" holds true so often when it comes to our feet.

I want to challenge you to consider those things in your marriage to which you pay minimal attention, but which definitely could use more attention. Do you say "please" and "thank you"? Do you ask your spouse's opinions? Do you spend quality time together? I truly believe that more attention in those areas can bring you much needed satisfaction and relief, much like an overdue foot massage. If you apply this simple yet significant principle to your marriage, you will find that you will be happier but your spouse will be happier too. In turn, the smile on your face and your partner's face will be priceless and unforgettable. Trust me, it works!

Whether you wear sandals, sneakers, shoes, or slippers your feet are valuable to you. Once you pay better attention to the neglected components of your marriage, your marriage walk will be much smoother. My hope for you is that your marriage will reach new levels of fulfillment. Don't hesitate to invest the love, time, energy, and money necessary to make your marriage a success.

Prayer

Dear Lord, I thank you for seeing me beyond my surface. I'm humbly asking that you would help me to give each area of my marriage the careful attention it needs. Help me to minimize and maximize where needed. In Jesus' name. Amen!

Scripture Focus

*You were faithful with a few things, I will put you in charge of many things... — **Matthew 25:21 (NASB)***

WORKBOOK

Chapter 10 Questions

Question: Today's reading, made me think about...

_____

_____

_____

_____

_____

_____

_____

_____

_____

_____

_____

Question: One thing I learned today is...

_____

_____

_____

_____

_____

_____

_____

_____

_____

_____

_____

_____

Action: Write down one specific way you will work to strengthen a neglected area of your marriage on a daily or regular basis.

_____

_____

_____

_____

Chapter 10 Notes

_____

_____

_____

_____

_____

_____

_____

_____

_____

_____

_____

_____

_____

_____

_____

_____

_____

_____

_____

_____

_____

_____

_____

_____

CHAPTER 11

Dumbbell, Barbells, and Cardio

It is a proven fact that if one wants to get physically stronger, resistance is necessary. Whether it be in the form of push-ups or pull ups, our muscles grow and develop when they experience resistance. In most fitness gyms, you will find lots of trendy and sophisticated forms of equipment. One of the reasons fitness centers provide such a wide variety of fitness machines is to help patrons target certain muscles when training. In addition, having a diversity of equipment helps customers refrain from becoming bored in the gym. However, one thing I have noticed living in various states and being a member of different gyms is all of them have dumbbells, barbells, and cardio equipment. It is my assumption that gyms realize trendy machines come and go but dumbbells and barbells are here to stay.

I share this interesting observation about dumbbells and barbells to say although marriages change due to time and experiences, there are certain fundamental basics about marriage that will never go away. Some of these marriage basics include: love, respect, communication, compassion, and compromise just to name a few. However, one of the fundamental basics that are essential for growth in one's marriage is resistance. In fact, resistance is quite normal. At some point in time, every single marriage will experience turbulence, resistance, opposition, and tension. Hence when your marriage encounters a season of resistance, see it as a season of growth designed to make your marriage stronger. Let's face it…No one likes resistance, opposition, pressure, or stress in their marriage but it is necessary for growth. Just like a trip to the gym results in sweat, resistance, and an occasional grunt, you endure it because you know it will pay off in the end.

Prayer

Dear God, I simply want to thank you for making sure the positive, affirming, and constructive components of my marriage outweigh the negative, challenging, and difficult parts of my marriage. Help us to become stronger today than we've been before. In Jesus' name. Amen!

Scripture Focus

And we know that in all things God works for the good of those who love him, who have been called according to his purpose. — **Romans 8:28 (NIV)**

WORKBOOK

Chapter 11 Questions

Question: Today's reading, made me think about...

_____

_____

_____

_____

_____

_____

_____

_____

_____

_____

_____

_____

Question: One thing I learned today is...

_____

_____

_____

_____

_____

_____

_____

_____

_____

_____

_____

_____

Action: Take time today to send your spouse a text message and to encourage them by letting them know that you trust that God will see you through the good times and the times that create resistance.

Chapter 11 Notes

_____

_____

_____

_____

_____

_____

_____

_____

_____

_____

_____

_____

_____

_____

_____

_____

_____

_____

_____

_____

_____

_____

_____

CHAPTER 12

Barricades and Bridges

Have you ever started out driving towards a particular destination only to be redirected because of a "barricade"? Sometimes these "barricades" come in the form of a car accident, road construction, traffic congestion, or fallen tree. In these instances, it is very easy to become angry, frustrated, and impatient because our travel time is delayed and extended. Unfortunately, situations like this can bring out the worst in us, if we let them. However, there are some positive ways to look at "barricades."

Sometimes, "barricades" are simply a means to reroute us in a different direction or as tools to help us avoid potentially hazardous situations. Similarly, "bridges" are designed to help us reach our destination by providing us with an overpass. Sometimes, these bridges take us over bodies of water, roadways, railroads, and other obstacles. If the truth be told, there are certain destinations that would not be reached, if bridges did not exist.

Barricades and bridges can exist in the context of marriage. As you consider the length of your marriage and some of the difficult situations you have encountered, just remember that some of these situations were barricades and some were bridges. Although it seems like life's barricades hinder, hamper, and hold up our progress, they actually benefit us more than we realize.

Sometimes we are in such a hurry to reach our destination that God has to present us with barricades in order to slow us down, reroute us, or to help us avoid hazardous situations. Hence, God places bridges in our lives to help us overpass and overcome life's obstacles. As you encounter the barricades and bridges together in your marriage, God is strengthening your relationship with your spouse. Just remember for every barricade, God can produce a bridge.

Today, use this metaphor of "barricades" and "bridges" as means to encourage yourself and your spouse through this week's challenges and victories.

Prayer

Lord, help us to remember that while we may make plans, you direct our path. Let us follow the leading of your Holy Spirit at all times so that we can fulfill your will for our lives. In Jesus' name. Amen!

Scripture Focus

In all your ways acknowledge him, and he will make straight your paths. — **Proverbs 3:6 (ESV)**

WORKBOOK

Chapter 12 Questions

Question: Today's reading, made me think about…

_____

_____

_____

_____

_____

_____

_____

_____

_____

_____

_____

Question: One thing I learned today is…

_____

_____

_____

_____

_____

_____

_____

_____

_____

_____

_____

_____

Action: Take time to talk with your spouse and together list some ways that God has protected, strengthened, or blessed you with a barricade or bridge.

Chapter 12 Notes

_____

_____

_____

_____

_____

_____

_____

_____

_____

_____

_____

_____

_____

_____

_____

_____

_____

_____

_____

_____

_____

_____

_____

_____

CHAPTER 13

Good News for Tough Times

Wouldn't it be nice if we didn't have to experience "tough times"? However the reality is tough times, trials, tribulations, and tests are a part of life. They never come at convenient times or at expected times. In addition, tough times rarely come in isolation. What's interesting about "tough times" is no one is exempt from having to deal with them. "Tough times" are certain to show up in our lives regardless of one's gender, age, nationality, educational attainment, or financial stability. Tough times are sure to show up in our careers, families, finances, communities, health, churches, and even marriages.

So the question is not if "tough times" will show up in your life but when. We know challenges are inevitable, imminent, and inescapable. However the question is, "how will you handle tough times when they show up?"

Although we would love for our marriages to be perfect, pleasant, and problem-free all the time, this is not reality. So when tough times show up, do you shut down? Do you become argumentative? Do you overeat? Do you over sleep? Do you isolate yourself? Do you pray to God? Do you study your Bible? Do you talk it over with your spouse? Do you seek counseling? Do you develop a healthy plan? Learn to identify and correct any negative patterns so the next time a challenge arises, you and your spouse will be better equipped.

The point here is simply to expect tough times and learn how to handle tough times. The good news is "tough times don't last always." Tough times are like the months on our calendars, they eventually move on. Tough times may also be likened to the seasons in nature; they eventually change. Hence, the key is not to panic or grow anxious in tough times.

Prayer

Lord, you are incredible, I just want to thank you for seeing us through tough times and for being with us at all times. We love you, Lord! In Jesus' name. Amen!

Scripture Focus

In the world ye shall have tribulation: but be of good cheer; I have overcome the world. — ***John 16:33 (KJV)***

WORKBOOK

Chapter 13 Questions

Question: Today's reading, made me think about...

_____

_____

_____

_____

_____

_____

_____

_____

_____

_____

_____

Question: One thing I learned today is...

_____

_____

_____

_____

_____

_____

_____

_____

_____

_____

_____

_____

Action: Encourage your spouse when tough times show up in your marriage. Pray together through the tough times. Remember, there is good news for tough times!

Chapter 13 Notes

_____

_____

_____

_____

_____

_____

_____

_____

_____

_____

_____

_____

_____

_____

_____

_____

_____

_____

_____

_____

_____

_____

_____

_____

CHAPTER 14

Build Your House Strategically

Anyone who has ever built a home or seen a home being built knows strategic planning is a key component of the home building process. In other words, there are certain strategic steps one must take before other steps are taken. For example, the land must be surveyed, a concrete foundation must be laid, and plumbing circulation must be determined just to name a few. Similarly, the house must be framed before it is fortified with cement blocks or bricks. In short, a poorly planned building process can be catastrophic for all involved. However, an intentional and deliberate building plan can be beautiful and beneficial to all involved.

Your marriage is just like a physical house which needs deliberate and intentional planning. A plan that outlines your short term goals and long term goals is always best. When was the last time you and your spouse sat down and mutually determined short term goals and long term goals for your marriage? Don't procrastinate when it comes to marriage planning. Remember, procrastination is the enemy of progress. Unfortunately, so many couples plan more for their wedding than they do their marriage.

My goal today is to inspire you and your spouse to set goals in the areas of your faith, family, finances, fitness, future, friends, and fun. What areas could be improved? What areas can you work on together? Setting goals for your marriage and planning for the future will be one of the wisest things you will ever do.

Prayer

Oh gracious Sustainer of Life, I acknowledge you today as the master builder. Thank you for helping my spouse and I build a meaningful life together. Help us to make good decisions that will line up with your perfect and holy will for our marriage. In Jesus' name. Amen!

Scripture Focus

By wisdom is a house built and by understanding is it established. — ***Proverbs 24:3 (NASB)***

WORKBOOK

Chapter 14 Questions

Question: Today's reading, made me think about...

_____

_____

_____

_____

_____

_____

_____

_____

_____

_____

_____

_____

Question: One thing I learned today is...

_____

_____

_____

_____

_____

_____

_____

_____

_____

_____

_____

_____

Action: Today, I encourage you and your spouse to begin writing down your short-term goals. Together come up with some specific ways to meet these goals.

Chapter 14 Notes

_____

_____

_____

_____

_____

_____

_____

_____

_____

_____

_____

_____

_____

_____

_____

_____

_____

_____

_____

_____

_____

_____

_____

_____

CHAPTER 15

Few Friends Formula

Friends are a blessing! In fact, all of us need friends. Life becomes more meaningful when we have true friends. You know, the kind of friends who make us laugh, challenge us, and inspire us.

The probability is high you and your spouse had other friends before the two of you even met. Perhaps these friends were past neighbors, classmates, or coworkers. However, the danger of investing your time in too many friends is it can drain your energy level and take away from your marriage. Friends can be a blessing or burden. Do you have friends your spouse doesn't like? Does your spouse have friends you don't like? Do you need to create space between you and your friends? Do you wish your spouse invited more friends in to their life? Whatever you decide, it has been my experience and training that having a small circle of close friends is always beneficial and manageable.

The advantages of having a small circle of friends is: you can hold one another accountable, strengthen relationships, share fun times together, laugh with one another, and cry together. Furthermore, I would encourage you and your spouse to develop friendships with other Christian couples in a mentoring relationship.

I am of the conviction that every couple ought to have an elder couple by whom they can be mentored or after whom they can model themselves. In addition, I believe every couple ought to be mentoring a younger couple. To this point, we see countless examples of mentor/mentee relationships throughout the Bible. For example, in the Old Testament we see Moses' mentorship by Jethro and Moses' mentorship to Joshua and Caleb. In the New Testament, we see it in Paul's mentorship by Gamliel and Paul's mentorship to Timothy and Titus. The point here is simple: every couple can learn something from another couple and every couple ought to be teaching another couple something of value.

Prayer

Dear God, I acknowledge you today as Jehovah Jireh, the God who provides. I ask that you would reveal to my spouse and I, the couple whom you would like to mentor us and disclose to us which couple you would like us to mentor. In Jesus' name. Amen!

Scripture Focus

That the aged men be sober, grave, temperate, sound in faith, in charity, in patience. The aged women likewise, that they be in behavior as becometh holiness, not false accusers, not given to much wine, teachers of good things; That they may teach the young women to be sober, to love their husbands, to love their children... — **Titus 2:2-4 (KJV)**

Chapter 15 Questions

Question: Today's reading, made me think about…

_____
_____
_____
_____
_____
_____
_____
_____
_____
_____
_____

Question: One thing I learned today is…

_____
_____
_____

_____

_____

_____

_____

_____

_____

_____

_____

_____

Action: With your spouse identify a "mentor couple" and identify a "mentee couple."

Chapter 15 Notes

CHAPTER 16

Instructions Not Included

Have you ever purchased or received a new microwave, washing machine, smartphone, or DVR? Was there an instruction manual or website included in the packaging? Most manufacturers spend a lot of time writing out detailed instructions for their products so their consumers/users can have an enjoyable and effective experience. The beauty of having an instruction manual is its usefulness transcends the initial use of the product and often serves as a reference guide for future troubleshooting. After all, we know there is nothing worse than having a problem with an item or device and not having the manual to coach you through your problem.

Unlike appliances or technological gadgets, children don't come with instructions. This idiom takes on new meaning when one has children of their own. Unlike a new microwave, washing machine, smartphone, or DVR, "children absolutely positively don't come with instructions." Thus, parenting becomes for many people one of the most fulfilling and demanding jobs they will ever experience.

Becoming a parent can affect your marriage in ways you cannot imagine. Regardless of your child's age, parenting can add both joy and stress to a marriage. However, the good news is parents don't have to solely rely on their own personal experiences, but can rely on the experiences of others. Here is another example of how a parental mentor can be invaluable. Hence, if you have been blessed with children or surrogate children, I want to encourage you to learn from the experiences of others. It is absolutely imperative that you and your spouse find a way to agree on parenting choices even if you have different parenting styles. This alone will reduce parenting-related stress on your marriage.

I challenge you to see parenting as a lifelong responsibility regardless of your child's age. In addition, you should see your learning as a parent as a lifelong endeavor. In short, you can never retire from parenting and never cease from learning. As you continue on your journey as a parent, God will strengthen you and your spouse as a couple and as parents.

Prayer

Lord, thank you for blessing us to be parents to your little children. Although they don't come with instructions, give us the instruction that we need. In Jesus' name. Amen!

Scripture Focus

The fear of the LORD is the beginning of knowledge: but fools despise wisdom and instruction. My son, hear the instruction of thy father, and forsake not the law of thy mother... — **Proverbs 1:7-8 (KJV)**

Chapter 16 Questions

Question: Today's reading, made me think about...

_____

_____

_____

_____

_____

_____

_____

_____

_____

_____

_____

Question: One thing I learned today is...

_____

_____

_____

_____

_____

_____

_____

_____

_____

_____

_____

_____

Action: (1) Write down three of the most important values you have regarding parenting. (2) Verbally share these values/standards with your spouse. (3) Then discuss how you will incorporate all these values in your parenting years.

_____

_____

_____

_____

Chapter 16 Notes

_____

_____

_____

_____

_____

_____

_____

_____

_____

_____

_____

_____

_____

_____

_____

_____

_____

_____

_____

_____

_____

_____

_____

CHAPTER 17

Early Bird or Night Owl

Are you an "early bird" or a "night owl"? Well before you answer too quickly, I have found that people are generally early birds regarding certain activities and night owls regarding other activities. For example there are some people who prefer working out in the morning versus the evening. There are some people, who enjoy watching the evening news versus the morning news. There are some who enjoying driving long distances early in the morning and some who prefer to drive long distances at night. I'm sure by now, you get the point. In short, there are some things you prefer to do at certain times of the day.

Believe it or not, there are certain aspects of your marriage that work better for your spouse early in the morning versus late at night. For example, some people like to resolve conflicts at night before going to bed and there are some who prefer to sleep on it and discuss it in the morning. There are some spouses who prefer to have sex at night versus in the morning, or in the morning versus at night. The point is, each of us have different rhythms about certain things. Hence, I want to encourage you to have some fun with your spouse and complete the "action step" below. Today, you will gain so much insight in to your spouse's early-bird or owl-like timing and nature.

Prayer

God, you are amazing, awesome, and all that! You made me as you saw fit and did the same for my mate. Help us to sync our rhythms, blend our tempos, and merge our pulses. Help us to respect our differences, admire our uniqueness, appreciate our variances, and celebrate our distinctiveness. Help us to see the beauty in one another, splendor in our talents, and brilliance in our creativity. Do something amazing, awesome, and all that is us. In Jesus' name. Amen!

Scripture Focus

...a season, and a time to every purpose under the heaven... — Ecclesiastes 3:1 (KJV)

WORKBOOK

Chapter 17 Questions

Question: Today's reading, made me think about…

_____

_____

_____

_____

_____

_____

_____

_____

_____

_____

_____

_____

Question: One thing I learned today is…

_____

_____

_____

_____

_____

_____

_____

_____

_____

_____

_____

_____

Action: Create a list with two columns, label one column early bird and the other column night owl. In one column write down five things you prefer to do in the morning and in the other column write down five things you prefer to do in the evening. Share your lists with one another, determine how well you know your spouse, and laugh about the "early bird" or "night owl" qualities you share.

Chapter 17 Notes

CHAPTER 18

When One Settles, All Suffer

When one settles for less, one usually ends up suffering! This single statement could easily be used as a dissertation topic, newspaper article, or small group Bible study series. Life is full of choices, decisions, and compromises. However, when one settles for less, he or she usually ends up regretting the decision they have made. All of us realize no one wins one-hundred percent of the time. However, settling causes one to lose every time. Settling for less than your standards just to obtain an easy fix or to make someone else happy must be avoided all costs. The reason I caution you about the dangers of settling is because it usually breeds resentment, anger, and bitterness over time.

By now, most of us have figured out one of the keys to a successful marriage is the ability to communicate and compromise. However, I want to argue that the danger and detriment to so many marriages is the cycle of settling. This cycle of settling is when one or both persons gets in the routine of lowering their standards and principles. This cycle of settling is particularly paralyzing when one spouse enables the other spouse by excusing poor habits, behavior, actions, and even mindsets.

Perhaps there are some things in your relationship that you have settled for and you want to break the cycle of settling in this specific area. I would like to encourage you to lovingly share your frustrations with your spouse and hopes for a brighter future. Please keep in mind this is not an easy conversation to have and requires much prayer. Allow the Holy Spirit to lead you and speak through you when having this difficult conversation. By addressing this sensitive area of your relationship, you will put yourself and your relationship on the path of greater fulfillment.

Prayer

Dear God guide me and direct me. I no longer want to settle but want your best for our marriage! Help me to say the words I need to say to my spouse so I don't foster resentment and our marriage can become healthier. In Jesus' name. Amen!

Scripture Focus

For the Holy Ghost shall teach you in the same hour what ye ought to say. — *Luke 12:12 (KJV)*

WORKBOOK

Chapter 18 Questions

Question: Today's reading, made me think about…

_____
_____
_____
_____
_____
_____
_____
_____
_____
_____
_____
_____

Question: One thing I learned today is…

_____
_____
_____

_____

_____

_____

_____

_____

_____

_____

_____

_____

_____

Action: Talk with your spouse about the areas of your marriage where you have both settled for less; then identify at least one of these areas in which you each hope to improve.

Chapter 18 Notes

_____

_____

_____

_____

_____

_____

_____

_____

_____

_____

_____

_____

_____

_____

_____

_____

_____

_____

_____

_____

_____

_____

_____

_____

CHAPTER 19

Intentional Intimacy

Very few things in life just happen! However, there are many things in life that happen with intentionality! Most people who have lost weight will tell you they did it intentionally. In the same breadth, many people who have saved money, will tell you they did so intentionally. The point here is very simple and straightforward: more is achieved when a person pursues his or her goal with intentionality.

Maintaining a healthy level of intimacy doesn't just automatically happen in a marriage. Both partners must be intentional and communicate with one another. Today, I want you to grade your level of intentional intimacy with your spouse. Do you intentionally set time aside to be intimate with your spouse? How intentional are you when it comes to pleasing him or her? Are you intentional about trying new things? Do you feel that your spouse is intentional when it comes to intimacy?

Are you satisfied with your level of intimacy you share with your spouse? Do you want to increase the frequency you are intimate with one another? Has your sex life become boring, predictable, and dull? Have you expressed to your spouse the things you like when being intimate? Has your sex life gotten better or worse with time? What could you do to make it better?

On the flip side, are you fulfilled in your sex life with your spouse? Do you believe it is possible to be intimate and not have sex? Are you intentionally a lover and pleaser to your spouse? Do you feel intimacy is overrated or downplayed? Do you allow your schedule, responsibilities, and obligations to interfere with intimacy with your mate? Regardless of your responses to these questions, work to intentionally improve the intimacy in your marriage.

Prayer

Oh Lord my God, thank you for being an intimate God who cares deeply about me. I desire to be more intimate with my spouse than ever before. Give us a fresh fire and fresh wind towards one another. In Jesus' name. Amen!

Scripture Focus

*Scarcely had I passed them when I found him whom my soul loves. I held him, and would not let him go... — **Song of Solomon 3:4 (ESV)***

WORKBOOK

Chapter 19 Questions

Question: Today's reading, made me think about…

_____

_____

_____

_____

_____

_____

_____

_____

_____

_____

_____

_____

Question: One think I learned today is…

_____

_____

_____

_____

_____

_____

_____

_____

_____

_____

_____

_____

Action: Shower your spouse with plenty of love for the next seven days. Overwhelm your spouse with seven consecutive days of romance, intimacy, and thoughtfulness.

Chapter 19 Notes

_____

_____

_____

_____

_____

_____

_____

_____

_____

_____

_____

_____

_____

_____

_____

_____

_____

_____

_____

_____

_____

_____

_____

_____

_____

CHAPTER 20

Vacation, Daycation, Staycation

Grab your calendar, day planner, appointment book, smartphone, laptop, or tablet and start planning now! Every couple needs to plan a vacation, daycation, and staycation. Just in case, you haven't heard of these terms before, allow me to explain. A vacation is a fun and relaxing trip that is scheduled miles away from your home for at least three days. A daycation is a pleasurable yet peaceful trip that is out of town yet close enough for you to drive back home in the same day. Finally, a staycation is an entertaining and delightful trip in your city or town that doesn't require extensive driving. Hence, I want to politely suggest you are doing your marriage a disservice, if are you are not regularly scheduling/taking vacations, daycations, and staycations with your spouse. However, the good news is you can change that today!

Every married couple needs to schedule spontaneous breaks from the rigors, regimes, and routines of life. The day to day grind of working, commuting, parenting, and cleaning has the potential to wear down even the greatest of people. Let's face it, life is good but life is hard! In the same breath, life is fun but it's not for the faint of heart. However, it you want to revitalize your marriage find the time to enjoy regular vacations, daycations, and staycations. This time alone and away will give you and your spouse an opportunity to reconnect on totally new levels. Always stay mindful life is short and tomorrow is not promised. Enjoy your spouse as much as you can and as often you can.

In conclusion, the Bible is replete with examples of Jesus taking breaks from the rigors, regimes, and routines of ministry. Jesus is a prime example to show us that our bodies, minds, and spirits need a break from the demands of others and the demands of life. A great illustration of Jesus taking a break to enjoy life is evident by His presence and participation at the wedding in Cana in John 2. Therefore, if Jesus Christ took time for breaks, then you should too!

Prayer

Heavenly father, thank you for showing me it is ok to take a break and rest. Please take away all feelings of guilt when I'm not working. Rejuvenate our marriage, O God, through vacations, daycations, and staycations. In Jesus' name. Amen!

Scripture Focus

*And God blessed the seventh day, and sanctified it: because that in it he had rested from all his work which God created and made. — **Genesis 2:4 (KJV)***

WORKBOOK

Chapter 20 Questions

Question: Today's reading, made me think about…

_____

_____

_____

_____

_____

_____

_____

_____

_____

_____

_____

Question: One think I learned today is…

_____

_____

_____

_____

_____

_____

_____

_____

_____

_____

_____

_____

Action: Today, sit down with your spouse and review your calendars. Your goal as a couple today is threefold: 1) clearly identify dates for a vacation, 2) determine a date and destination for your daycation, and 3) pinpoint a day that you will do a staycation.

Chapter 20 Notes

CHAPTER 21

Dealing with Childhood Issues

For years, I have theorized that "adults are grown folks dealing with childhood issues." It has been my observation and professional opinion as a Senior Pastor that every adult has some unresolved childhood issues. Whether we realize it or not, our childhoods impact us in profound and long-lasting ways. The impact of our childhood can be both, positive and negative. Everything from birth order, looks, parental validation, sibling rivalry, academic performance, abuse, neglect, death, divorce, and relocation can affect us as children and adults. Just think about it, have you ever met someone and wondered what happened in their childhood that causes them to behave the way they do as an adult? In the same breath, have you ever noticed your childhood has impacted you as an adult in subtle or overt ways? Interestingly enough, these childhood issues have an impact on our adult friendships, relationships, and marriage.

Today is going to be your day to do some introspection, reflection, and investigation in to your childhood. Although we can't relive the past, it is important and valuable to work through these issues with your spouse, your pastor, or a professional counselor. One's willingness to see a pastor, therapist, or counselor can make a difference in one's physical, mental, and spiritual health. The healthier you are as an individual, the healthier you will be for your marriage. Therefore, lay the unsettled troubles of your past to rest.

Prayer

Lord, thank you for giving us the gift of forgiveness. Help me today to be willing to be a courageous adult and deal with my childhood issues. Thank you in advance for working on my behalf. In Jesus' name. Amen!

Scripture Focus

Come unto me, all ye that labour and are heavy laden, and I will give you rest. — ***Matthew 11:28 (KJV)***

WORKBOOK

Chapter 21 Questions

Question: Today's reading, made me think about...

_____

_____

_____

_____

_____

_____

_____

_____

_____

_____

_____

_____

Question: One think I learned today is...

_____

_____

_____

_____

_____

_____

_____

_____

_____

_____

_____

Action: Your responsibility in the next twenty-four hours is to write down one thing from your childhood that has positively impacted you as an adult. In addition, write down one thing from childhood that may be negatively impacting you as an adult.

Chapter 21 Notes

_____

_____

_____

_____

_____

_____

_____

_____

_____

_____

_____

_____

_____

_____

_____

_____

_____

_____

_____

_____

_____

_____

_____

_____

_____

_____

_____

CHAPTER 22

Bud, Bloom, and Blossom

Every flower, plant, bush, shrub, or tree began as a seed! So often, we see each of these items in its mature or developed state, but rarely consider that it was once a seed. Hence, anyone who is familiar with agriculture, horticulture, botany, farming, or gardening knows there are five keys to a seed's growth. A seed's growth is often determined by the soil, the sower, sunlight, the season, and the supply of water. The beauty is seeds have figured out how to grow where they are planted. In other words, they figure out how to maximize and develop where are. Yes, there are ideal places to grow and develop but we all have to make a decision to grow where we are planted. As a result, it's just a matter of time before those seeds begin to bud, bloom, and blossom.

In marriage, we are challenged to grow where we are planted. This may mean growing in the city you live, in the job you occupy, or in the family you have been placed in. The key is to grow and to grow without excuses. Life is too short to make excuses and life is too short to be stagnant. Know you are a precious seed in the eyes of God and God wants you to grow where He plants you because He has a purpose for you. In the same breath, God wants you (the sower) to plant seeds in good soil so you may grow in due season. By accepting the challenge of growing where you are planted, then you can be encouraged by your spouse in your endeavors as you all share the ups and downs of life.

Sometimes, God places us in certain settings and situations to stimulate our growth. Sometimes these settings and situations are uncomfortable, undesirable, unfriendly, and unpleasant. Nonetheless, make up in your mind you are going to grow wherever you are planted. By learning to be faithful, fruitful, and fertile wherever you are planted, you are positioning yourself to be blessed by God.

To sum it all up, most of us are rarely in a perfect or ideal situation but we must learn to make the best of every situation. Finally, make a commitment to work on this aspect of your life and ask God to bless you where you are.

Prayer

Dear Lord, help me to bud, bloom, and blossom where you have placed me. Today, I will meditate on the parable of the seeds as told by Jesus in Matthew 13:3-9. In Jesus' name. Amen!

Scripture Focus

Other seeds fell on good soil and produced grain, some a hundredfold, some sixty, some thirty. — ***Matthew 13:8 (KJV)***

WORKBOOK

Chapter 22 Questions

Question: One thing I learned today is...

_____

_____

_____

_____

_____

_____

_____

_____

_____

_____

_____

Action: Pinpoint and share with your spouse one area of your life you would like to be improved. In doing this exercise, it's important to identify a component of your life that you actually have control or agency over. Then ask your spouse to help you think through ways you can grow where you are planted as it relates to that component of your life.

Chapter 22 Notes

_____

_____

_____

_____

_____

_____

_____

_____

_____

_____

_____

_____

_____

_____

_____

_____

_____

_____

_____

_____

_____

CHAPTER 23

Power Couple or Impactful Couple

Each year various magazines print and publish what they call their "100 most powerful people" list. Each year, you will find it is not uncommon or unusual to see the names of men and women who are national leaders, CEO's, entertainers, politicians, pastors, or philanthropists, just to name a few on these lists. As one would expect, some of the most powerful, prominent, and popular people of our day are placed on these lists.

I want to submit and suggest to you that just because one is "powerful," it doesn't necessarily mean one is "impactful." Those who are typically labeled as "powerful" are usually persons with authority. However, what good is one's authority if one doesn't use his or her authority in positive and progressive ways? Whereas when one aims to be impactful, they search for ways to be transformative and ways to enhance the lives of others. Now it is possible to be both powerful and impactful. However, the majority of people endeavor to be powerful versus impactful. This is unfortunate but can be redeemed.

In the same breath, there are many husbands and wives who aspire to be a "power couple" instead of being an "impactful couple." Hence in my humble opinion, I believe it is more meaningful and valuable when a couple aspires to be an "impactful couple." The actuality is we have enough "power couples" in the world but we need more "impactful couples" in the world. The world needs more couples who will positively impact their communities and cities. In every community there are schools, financial institutions, civic organizations, hospitals, recreational centers, churches, and businesses that would love to have an "impact couple" in their midst who is committed to making a difference in the lives of others.

Prayer

Our Lord and Creator, help us to be an impactful couple. Show us what you desire for us to do. Empower us to make an impact on your behalf in our community and in our church. In Jesus' name. Amen!

Scripture Focus

Though one person may be overpowered by another, two people can resist one opponent. A triple-braided rope is not easily broken. — Ecclesiastes 4:12 (GWT)

Chapter 23 Questions

Question: Today's reading, made me think about…

_____

_____

_____

_____

_____

_____

_____

_____

_____

_____

_____

Question: One thing I learned today is…

_____

_____

_____

_____

_____

_____

_____

_____

_____

_____

_____

_____

Action: Today, I want you to discuss with your spouse the idea of being an "impactful couple" and not just a "powerful couple." Begin the process of exploring places and ways you can make an immediate and long-term impact. I promise you this will be one of the most fulfilling decisions you will ever make as couple.

Chapter 23 Notes

_____

_____

_____

_____

_____

_____

_____

_____

_____

_____

_____

_____

_____

_____

_____

_____

_____

_____

_____

_____

_____

_____

_____

_____

_____

_____

CHAPTER 24

Toilet Tissue and Paper Towels

Have you ever visited the restroom and discovered all the toilet tissue or paper towels were gone? I know this may strike you as an odd and rather direct question. However, this is a real question and very practical question. If we are honest, it's not unrealistic or unreasonable to expect restrooms to be stocked with toilet tissue and paper towels at all times. However, having a restroom that is stocked with toilet tissue and paper towels is one of those conveniences we take for granted until it is not in place. I utilize this real-life example to highlight the fact that there are so many things we expect and take for granted in marriage. Interestingly, we all know there are some things that happen only because someone else was willing to pay attention to the details. Expecting someone else to stock the restroom with toilet tissue and paper towels is one of those conveniences we expect and take for granted.

Today, take some time to assess the things you expect your spouse to do but often take for granted. I guarantee you there are chores, errands, tasks, duties, and responsibilities he or she carries out that you take for granted. Regularly recognizing the value your spouse brings to your marriage is valuable. In the same breath, when you, verbally, let your spouse know you appreciate them it is even more valuable. So the next time your spouse restocks the restroom with toilet tissue or paper towels, please don't hesitate to let them know you appreciate them. I know it seems small and even comical, but trust me it will go a long way. The simple lesson here is, when you compliment your spouse on the small things, it will be much easier to appreciate them with all the other chores, errands, tasks, duties, and responsibilities they carry out.

Prayer

Dear Lord, I thank you for the people you have sent into my life and help me to thank them for all they do to inspire me. In Jesus' name. Amen!

Scripture Focus

I always thank my God for you because of his grace given you in Christ Jesus. — 1 Corinthians 1:4 (NIV)

WORKBOOK

Chapter 24 Questions

Question: Today's reading, made me think about…

_____

_____

_____

_____

_____

_____

_____

_____

_____

_____

_____

Question: One thing I learned today is…

_____

_____

_____

_____

_____

_____

_____

_____

_____

_____

_____

_____

Action: As soon as you finish this chapter, call your spouse to thank them for being a valuable, irreplaceable, and significant part of your life. Begin a habit of thanking your spouse regularly for the small things.

Chapter 24 Notes

_____

_____

_____

_____

_____

_____

_____

_____

_____

_____

_____

_____

_____

_____

_____

_____

_____

_____

_____

_____

_____

_____

CHAPTER 25

Small Steps, Big Strides

Don't base your marriage off of reality TV! Reality TV is fun to watch and even entertaining, to say the least. However, someone else's reality may not be your reality. Most reality TV shows present people/actors who appear to live great, grand, and glorious lives. The common images projected and perpetrated on your TV screen, include but are not limited to, the extravagant estates, luxury vehicles, exotic furs, majestic vacations, radiant jewelry, and tailor made wardrobes. However, this is only one side of the coin and doesn't paint the full picture. The other part of the picture, when viewing reality TV, highlights the disruptive dysfunction that exists in many of our lives. Always remember there is more to a person's story than what is told.

I mention this to say many people have been bamboozled into thinking success is easy and an entitlement for being a good person. On quite the contrary, success is a struggle and comes with a lot of sacrifice. Furthermore, success in a specific arena or field is often the result of small steps that turned in to big strides.

My hope is you are inspired today to take small steps towards your success. Know your small steps will turn into great strides with time. You and your husband/wife are in it for the long haul. Stay consistent, committed, and constant. Focus on your goals as a couple and work at it step by step. Keep working, keep grinding, and keep persevering! Small steps turn in to bigger strides!

Prayer

It is in the marvelous and mighty name of Jesus that I ask you to give me the courage to take the first step towards my goals. In addition, give me the courage and strength to continue the steps I stopped taking. Please give me a glimpse of the big picture and help me to see small steps do turn into big strides. In Jesus' name. Amen!

Scripture Focus

The steps of a good man are ordered by the LORD: and he delighteth in his way. — ***Psalm 37:23 (KJV)***

WORKBOOK

Chapter 25 Questions

Question: Today's reading, made me think about…

_____
_____
_____
_____
_____
_____
_____
_____
_____
_____
_____

Question: One thing I learned today is…

_____
_____
_____

_____

_____

_____

_____

_____

_____

_____

_____

_____

Action: Send an email to yourself stating one small step you are going to take towards your future.

Chapter 25 Notes

CHAPTER 26

Everybody Doesn't Have to Know

There are some things about your marriage and your spouse people should not know. So often we look to our friends and family to function as sounding boards or listening ears when it comes to the details of our lives. There are times when this is healthy and then there are times when this is unhealthy. It is healthy to know you have a safe place to go when you don't want to bombard, worry, or stress your spouse. However, the things we share with others in those delicate moments are usually sensitive and vulnerable subject matters.

How many times have you found yourself repeating the same scenario to multiple friends? How many times have you found yourself discussing the outcome of a situation to several people? Finally, how often do you find yourself entertaining questions about your past, present, or future? Choose carefully who you share information with.

Just remember everyone doesn't need to know your business or the details of your life. Unfortunately, there are instances when people divulge information that was supposed to be confidential. By now, you should know who you can and cannot trust. When in doubt about what to share and with whom, learn to pray about it and trust your instincts. The old adage still holds true, "loose lips, sinks ships." Don't allow loose lips to sink your marriage ship.

Your marriage is too valuable and prized to be handled haphazardly by loose lips. Your coworkers, siblings, parents, church members, fraternity brothers, and sorority sisters should not know all the inner workings of your household or marriage. There will be times when you want to share with others but will have to keep it inside instead. Learn to be okay with that and keep looking ahead.

Prayer

Oh Divine and Holy Spirit, please grant me the discernment to determine how much to share about my marriage and with whom to share these details of my life. Keep my tongue from disrespecting my spouse or breaching the confidentiality of our marriage. In Jesus' name I pray. Amen!

Scripture Focus

Death and life are in the power of the tongue, and those who love it will eat its fruit." — ***Proverbs 18:21 (ESV)***

WORKBOOK

Chapter 26 Questions

Question: Today's reading, made me think about…

_____

_____

_____

_____

_____

_____

_____

_____

_____

_____

_____

Question: One thing I learned today is…

_____

_____

_____

_____

_____

_____

_____

_____

_____

_____

_____

_____

Action: Think about a time you shared too much of your business with someone. If you could turn back the hands of time, how would you have handled that situation differently?

Chapter 26 Notes

CHAPTER 27

Plan Now for Your Anniversary

Don't wait, plan now for your anniversary. In other words, it is never too early to plan for your wedding anniversary. Although you do exciting things all year for your spouse, your anniversary is the one time of year you can really put some major thought and resources into your special day. Your spouse deserves the best that your time, creativity, and heart has to offer. Keep in mind there are some things that work out best when they happen spontaneously. However, there are some things that work out best when planned well in advance. Whether your wedding anniversary is a month, five months, or ten months away, now is the perfect time to plan for your anniversary. Just as you and your spouse placed a lot of thought in to planning your wedding day, it is to your advantage to plan thoroughly for your anniversary. Just think about it, you will never regret planning well in advance for your wedding anniversary.

Dinners, movies, cruises, trips, rings, watches, earrings, necklaces, gift cards, lunches, breakfasts, manicures, pedicures, massages, manicures, pedicures, purses, wallets, clothes, shoes, perfumes, colognes, concert tickets, or comedy shows are just some of the ideas you can plan for well in advance. Remember, your spouse isn't necessarily interested in how much money you spend on your anniversary. Conversely, your spouse is interested in the amount of time and effort you put into planning your wedding anniversary.

Love is an action word and what better way to express your love to your spouse than by putting together a well thought out anniversary celebration. I truly believe that in planning this special day, you will become increasingly excited about your effort.

Prayer

Dear Sustainer of Life, your Word is very clear about loving your spouse as I love myself, allow my anniversary planning efforts to be a reflection of my love for my spouse. In Jesus' name. Amen!

Scripture Focus

So ought men to love their wives as their own bodies. He that loveth his wife loveth himself. — ***Ephesians 5:28 (KJV)***

WORKBOOK

Chapter 27 Questions

Question: Today's reading, made me think about…

_____

_____

_____

_____

_____

_____

_____

_____

_____

_____

_____

Question: One thing I learned today is…

_____

_____

_____

_____

_____

_____

_____

_____

_____

_____

_____

_____

Action: Take out a calendar and brainstorm ideas for your next anniversary.

Chapter 27 Notes

_____

_____

_____

_____

_____

_____

_____

_____

_____

_____

_____

_____

_____

_____

_____

_____

_____

_____

_____

_____

_____

_____

CHAPTER 28

The Treasure of "Talk Time"

There is nothing that compares to the warm, inviting, and joyful connection you experience from a heartfelt conversation with your spouse. Belonging to a fulfilling marriage is one of the best feelings in the world. One of the ways you can keep your marriage fulfilled is through regular, reflective, and respectful conversations. Communication is key in any relationship, but especially in a marriage. Communication helps to minimize confusion, chaos, and contention. In addition, communication helps to strengthen your understanding of your spouse and helps both of you stay on the same page. How would your spouse rate your communication skills? How would you rate your mate's communication skills?

Due to the fact that you and your spouse live busy lives, communication can be a challenge. However, your job as a faithful and committed spouse is to make communication a priority in your relationship. Talk about everything to one another. Talk about the good, bad, and ugly. Talk about things that are easy to discuss and hard to converse about. Talk about those things that are simple and complicated. Talk about those things that make you smile and cry. Talk about it, talk about it, and talk about it some more. Set aside time to talk. Schedule "talk time" like a work related appointment or like a doctor's appointment. When couples refuse to talk, they grow further and further apart. Grow closer to your spouse by talking. As a husband or as a wife, make it your daily duty to keep fresh wood on the fire called marriage through communication. A cold marriage is never fun.

Prayer

Dear Ruler of the Universe, help me to become a better communicator with my spouse. Help me to create time to communicate and help me to be a better listener. Most importantly, help me to better communicate with you. In Jesus' name. Amen!

Scripture Focus

Kind words are like honey—sweet to the soul and healthy for the body. — **Proverbs 16:24 (NLT)**

Chapter 28 Questions

Question: Today's reading, made me think about…

_____

_____

_____

_____

_____

_____

_____

_____

_____

_____

_____

Question: One thing I learned today is…

_____

_____

_____

_____

_____

_____

_____

_____

_____

_____

_____

_____

Action: Contact your spouse and schedule a time/appointment just to talk.

Chapter 28 Notes

_____

_____

_____

_____

_____

_____

_____

_____

_____

_____

_____

_____

_____

_____

_____

_____

_____

_____

_____

_____

_____

_____

_____

CHAPTER 29

Spectacular Surprises

Everyone likes surprises! Some may not admit it, but when we're surprised with a gift we have wanted for some time, we tend to get over our dislike for surprises. Generally we present our spouse with big gifts only on special days or holidays. Most of us would agree that Valentine's Day, our wedding anniversary, Mother's Day, Father's Day, and Christmas are the predictable big gift-giving days. Nonetheless, most of us would agree the best gifts come when we least expect it.

Today, your goal is to surprise your spouse with an unexpected gift. The size and magnitude of your unexpected gift is totally up to you. However, I would like to encourage you to lean towards doing something bigger than normal and call it a "just because gift." We name it this because your spouse is going to wonder what they did to earn their unexpected gift, just tell them it is their "just because gift."

As I crisscross the country sharing with married couples and observing them, I have noticed so many marriages become dull and dry over time. It is my assessment too many couples have become too comfortable with the flow of their marriage. These marriages are predictable and lack spontaneity. Many marriages need the occasional surprise element. In other instances, many marriages have become convoluted by the stresses of marriage. If you have ever noticed a wood burning fire, you will notice as long as the firewood stays ablaze it creates a flame. However, when a fire lacks wood and oxygen, it eventually burns out and extinguishes itself. With this in mind, when was the last time you placed fresh wood on your marriage fire? How would your spouse describe your marriage flame? Is it burning bright or burning out? How can you surprise your spouse?

Eventually, you and your spouse will no longer see "just because gifts" as a duty but a delight! From today forward, bless your partner with spectacular surprises.

Prayer

Dear Lord, thank you for the reminder to bless and surprise my spouse continually. Please help me find ways to please my spouse and to bring them additional joy. In Jesus' name. Amen!

Scripture Focus

The husband should fulfill his marital duty to his wife, and likewise the wife to her husband. — *1 Corinthians 7:3 (NIV)*

WORKBOOK

Chapter 29 Questions

Question: Today's reading, made me think about…

_____
_____
_____
_____
_____
_____
_____
_____
_____
_____
_____
_____

Question: One thing I learned today is…

_____
_____
_____

_____

_____

_____

_____

_____

_____

_____

_____

_____

Action: Bless your husband or wife with a "just because gift" today. Your "spectacular surprise" will place a huge smile on their face.

Chapter 29 Notes

_____

_____

_____

_____

_____

_____

_____

_____

_____

_____

_____

_____

_____

_____

_____

_____

_____

_____

_____

_____

_____

_____

_____

CHAPTER 30

Taking Care of Business

We all have heard it before: "No Finance, No Romance"! I can't tell you exactly who coined this phrase but I can tell you they knew what they were talking about. Perhaps the author of this idiom spoke from personal experience or from the complaints of others. The reality is when couples consistently deal with uncertain financially stability, it affects all aspects of their relationship. I cannot scientifically say for certain what happens when one experiences financial, fiscal, or fiduciary hardship. However, I can say with complete confidence that economic hardship negatively impacts marriages and intimacy.

On the flip side, when the financial picture is intact, couples tend to feel closer to one another and much more fulfilled. There are not nearly as many arguments, disagreements, or quarrels when the money is flowing freely. Having a financial game plan is so important and makes the marriage flow so freely. If you follow the guidelines in this chapter's action plan, you will be off to a solid start in this area.

Prayer

Dear God, I thank you for being a God of abundance. I've read in your Word that you "own cattle on a thousand hills." Today, I need you to provide for my spouse and I. We have bills that are due, obligations to fulfill, responsibilities to uphold, and a household to maintain. Show us how to plan better, spend less, save more, and invest wisely. Show us those financial areas we need to improve and affirm us in those fiscal areas we are doing well. Help us to leave a monetary inheritance for the next generation. Give us the courage to share our financial struggles with others and to discuss money management with our families. Help us to be generous givers and faithful stewards. Give us hearts that do more than the tithe. Help us keep our eyes on you and not on money. In closing, we recognize we are blessed because of your mercy and love towards us. In Jesus' name. Amen!

Scripture Focus

*For which of you, intending to build a tower, sitteth not down first, and counteth the cost, whether he have sufficient to finish it? — **Luke 14:28 (KJV)***

WORKBOOK

Chapter 30 Questions

Question: Today's reading, made me think about…

_____

_____

_____

_____

_____

_____

_____

_____

_____

_____

_____

Question: One thing I learned today is…

_____

_____

_____

_____

_____

_____

_____

_____

_____

_____

_____

_____

Action: Take specific steps toward financial stability in your marriage. For instance, make a living will and get a life insurance policy. Set a budget and deposit money into your savings account regularly. Check your credit score, too, and write out how you will minimize your debt over the next six months.

Chapter 30 Notes

CHAPTER 31

In Sickness and in Health

Some of the most memorable and powerful words repeated during a marriage ceremony are "for richer, for poorer, for better, for worse, and in sickness and health." These vows are often expressed by the groom and bride in a moment of bliss and euphoria. However, the reality of these promises don't always sink in until one is actually living it.

Can you truly love your spouse while focusing on your own illness? How might your spouse's health problems test your commitment to your nuptials? How will you and your spouse handle a chronic illness or injury if it arises? When someone is in constant pain, then they are not always the most cheerful to get along with. Can you still love when cancer, disability, or age makes daily life and physical intimacy more difficult?

Honestly, it would be nice to know everything that will happen in your marriage ahead of time but the reality is only God knows. In addition, it would be nice to say how you are going to react to every situation that arises in your marriage but the truth is you don't know how you are going to respond until you are in it. Life is full of unexpected twists and turns, peaks and valleys.

We all know our bodies are not meant to last forever and are decaying daily, hence it is worthwhile to consider our own humanity and mortality. It has been my observation, that many couples face these questions and scenarios sooner than they would like. Unfortunately, many never talk over these facts of life until they happen.

I want to encourage you to appreciate, savor, and relish every moment with your spouse because life can change for you over night. In the same breath, it is good to have spent some intentional time talking about the unpleasant realities of life before they occur.

Prayer

Lord, you have smiled on me! Thank you for blessing me with a spouse who loves me for me. I know I'm not perfect and even difficult to deal with at times. But my spouse and you love me anyway. Strengthen our commitment to you and to one another. In Jesus' name. Amen!

Scripture Focus

*What therefore God hath joined together, let not man put asunder. — **Mark 10:9 (KJV)***

WORKBOOK

Chapter 31 Questions

Question: Today's reading, made me think about...

_____

_____

_____

_____

_____

_____

_____

_____

_____

_____

_____

Question: One thing I learned today is...

_____

_____

_____

_____

_____

_____

_____

_____

_____

_____

_____

_____

Action: Research your vows, reread your vows, and recommit yourself to your marriage.

Chapter 31 Notes

_____

_____

_____

_____

_____

_____

_____

_____

_____

_____

_____

_____

_____

_____

_____

_____

_____

_____

_____

_____

_____

_____

_____

CONCLUSION

Happily Ever After

It is my hope that you and your spouse will enjoy the remainder of your "happily ever after" days together. It is my prayer you and your spouse keep God first in all you do, individually and collectively. Finally, it is my hope the readings and activities of the past thirty-one days have transformed your life and marriage.

As you know by now, marriage is something that has to be worked at and worked on constantly. It is one of the best institutions ever created by God and will forever be the foundation of societies and communities around the world. Every day make it your duty to celebrate the one whom God has placed in your life. Pursue God's purpose for your lives together as a unit and as a team. Remember, God is with you and is willing to see you through.

About the Author

As a sought-after preacher, facilitator, and teacher, Dr. Berry uses his insights and humor to inspire people from all walks of life. Over the years, Dr. Berry has counseled, advised, and encouraged countless couples to healthier places in their relationship. Currently, Dr. Berry serves as the Senior Pastor/Teacher of Fourth Baptist Church in Richmond, Virginia, and is helping FBC grow to be a significant contributor to its membership and community. Dr. Berry received his undergraduate degree from the University of Florida, his master's degree from Emory University, and his doctorate degree from Virginia Union University. In addition, Dr. Berry has completed post-graduate studies at Harvard University, Princeton Theological Seminary, and Wake Forest University. He is most celebrated for being an approachable, personable, fun, and astute individual. He is married to Dr. Julie A. Berry, and they have been blessed with two wonderful children.

About Sermon To Book

SermonToBook.com began with a simple belief: that sermons should be touching lives, *not* collecting dust. That's why we turn sermons into high-quality books that are accessible to people all over the globe.

Turning your sermon series into a book exposes more people to God's Word, better equips you for counseling, accelerates future sermon prep, adds credibility to your ministry, and even helps make ends meet during tight times.

John 21:25 tells us that the world itself couldn't contain the books that would be written about the work of Jesus Christ. Our mission is to try anyway. Because, in Heaven, there will no longer be a need for sermons or books. Our time is now.

If God so leads you, we'd love to work with you on your sermon or sermon series.

Visit www.sermontobook.com to learn more.